A Trip to the Moon

By Cameron Macintosh

Contents

To the Moon!

A crew of people is going to the Moon!

On the way to the Moon, the crew will eat space food.

The crew put on space suits and boots.

PINCH POINT

Boom!

Up they go!

They'll cruise to the Moon in this spaceship.

It takes around three days to get there.

On the Moon

When they get there, the crew do some loops around the Moon.

Then they cruise down
to the Moon
in a small spaceship.

The crew has landed on the Moon!

They walk around in moon boots.

These are the best shoes for walking on the Moon.

There's a lot to do.

They scoop up loose rocks with tools as proof of the trip.

Back Home Again

It's soon time to fly back home.

The trip is smooth and safe.

They land in the blue sea
in a small pod.

The group at home is in a great mood!

Would you choose to go to the Moon?

CHECKING FOR MEANING

1. What will the crew eat on their trip? *(Literal)*
2. How do the crew get from their spaceship to the Moon? *(Literal)*
3. Why is the home group in a good mood? *(Inferential)*

EXTENDING VOCABULARY

crew	What is a crew? Where else might you find a crew?
cruise	Read the word *cruise*. What letters in this word make the /ū/ sound? What are some other words that the author could have used in the text instead of *cruise*?
loose	What does it mean if rocks are loose? If the rocks in the text weren't loose, could the astronaut have picked them up?

MOVING BEYOND THE TEXT

1. Would you like to visit the Moon? Why?
2. What equipment do you need to travel to the Moon? What do you think you would see if you were on the Moon?
3. How is the Moon different from Earth?
4. What are some other things that you can see in space?

TIME TO WRITE

Imagine you are one of the space crew that will land on the Moon. Write about how you feel when you first see the Moon from your spaceship, and what you will do on the Moon when you land.

PRACTICE WORDS

to

suits

do

tools

crew

boom

cruise

group

moon

food

scoop

proof

mood

boots

shoes

loose

choose

you

loops

soon

it's

smooth

blue

they'll

there's